For the feelers,
    thinkers, &
    dreamers.

# THE CREATIVE COPING TOOLKIT

by
Scilla Andreen

Illustrated by
Jerrin Padre

First paperback edition November 2019
Book design by Jerrin Padre
Illustrations copyright © Jerrin Padre 2019
Editorial: Jerrin Padre, Cole Weinstein & Natalie Andreen

ISBN: 978-1-7341990-0-0 (Paperback)
ISBN: 978-1-7341990-1-7 (eBook)

Published by IndieFlix Group, Inc.
www.creativecopingtoolkit.com

The CCT is a prevention tool and is not a replacement for therapy. Material presented in this book is for informational purposes only and is not intended to serve as a substitute for the consultation, diagnosis, or medical treatment of a qualified physician or healthcare provider. If you are in need of help, please contact the crisis text line, your primary care physician, or the national suicide prevention line.

Crisis Text Line
For US text 741741. For Canada text 686868.

National Suicide Prevention Lifeline
1-800-273-8255.

Available 24 hours every day.

# DEDICATION

This book is dedicated to my younger self, whose little heart, during the loneliest and toughest of times, was filled with so much love, compassion and forgiveness that it has become the foundation from which I draw all things.

# IMPACT

"The Creative Coping Toolkit is a beautifully simple, heart-warming approach to tackling some of the toughest issues we face growing up. We are taken by the hand and lightly walked through exercises like how to use language or art to express mood, or to effectively engage others in our journey to better connection. The reader is invited to create their own tools, and empowered to share ideas, thus building trust and resilience for future challenges. Scilla and Jerrin will surely touch the lives of many through this easy and accessible path to better mental health."

**Emily Y. Wong**, M.D., M.H.A., F.A.C.P.
Affiliate Associate Professor, Department of Medicine University of Washington (UW) Honorary Associate Professor, Department of Family Medicine and Primary Care University of Hong Kong (HKU)

———

"Per usual, Scilla is masterful at sparking important conversations among families. It's all too easy to zone out and avoid self-inquiry/reflection in our digitally driven world. Glad this book exists to help fight that trend."

**Max Stossel**, Head of Education
The Center for Humane Technology

"This toolkit is a creative, thoughtful and intelligently written gem for everyone navigating our increasingly complex world. It is refreshing to see such a book full of practical strategies grounded in theory and evidence yet shared in an insightful and simplistic way. This book should be on every child, adolescent and adult's bookshelf as it will without doubt have a positive impact on all those who pick it up and are inspired to use it. Scilla and Jerrin have created a toolkit masterpiece, I couldn't think of a more important and relevant topic for people today."

**Andrea Downie**, MAPP, BA (Psych), BEd
Co-founding Director of Project Thrive Australia,
Centre for Positive Psychology, University of Melbourne, Australia

———

"What an incredible gift you have delivered with this Creative Coping Toolkit. As a personal use tool, or as a conversation starter for families and friends, it's clear these are the tools we all need to be better — better individuals, better parents and better friends. As Dr. Jerry Bubrick stated, 35% of children will have a diagnosable anxiety disorder by the age of 18. It's our job to get engaged and start real conversations now. The exercises in this book provide a simple, approachable and thought provoking approach to understanding and being understood. Well done!!"

**Shelley Callaghan**, Creative Director/Owner
Antica Farmacista

"The world is changing fast, technology is everywhere, and politics are... well, politics. Now more than ever, we need to be talking about how we feel. Unfortunately, the things we need to talk most about are rarely the same as the things we want to discuss. Mental heath is important, yet stigmatized. Hard feelings are universal, though taught to be silenced. Scilla, through 10 brilliant exercises, bridges these gaps. She has managed to take unsung realities of everyday life and transform the discussions around them into approachable, manageable, dare I say fun, activities. If you've ever felt anxiety, this book is for you. If you've ever not known how to ask for help, this book is for you. If you or someone you know is a human on this earth, the Creative Coping Toolkit is a valuable resource you deserve in your life."

**Brendan Dunlap**, Recent College Graduate
B.A. Film & Media Studies, Whitman College

––––––

"Scilla is a preeminent voice in the movement of reconnecting people to themselves and each other."

**Jesse Israel**, Founder
The Big Quiet

"Just the act of reading this book brought happiness. As with her films, Scilla Andreen doesn't miss a beat in her empathetic and acute understanding of the nature of well-being. But what makes this book so helpful is that she translates that understanding into practical, simple tips and tools that anyone can put into practice to ease anxiety — for themselves and for their loved ones."

**Ruth Johnston**, General Manager
Vulcan Productions

———

"The Creative Coping Toolkit is an incredible book — actually it's much more than a book. It is a resource filled with ideas, suggestions and illustrations. It is written with an openness and thoughtfulness that just lets a reader in to the concept of feeling hopeful and whole, like a warm chocolate chip cookie straight out of the oven. The concepts are beautifully illustrated and the pages leave a space for one to use their own creative artistic energy. This is a "must have" toolkit and rightfully belongs in the library of parents/caregivers, teens and young adults, therapists, teachers and physicians."

**Cora Collette Breuner**, MD, MPH, FAAP
Professor, Department of Pediatrics and Adolescent Medicine;
Adjunct Professor, Orthopedics and Sports Medicine;
Seattle Children's Hospital, University of Washington

"We live in a world where technology and media continue to move faster than we can keep up, and it is ubiquitous. Despite the complexity of innovation, our behavior and decision making can provide a guiding foundation for how we leverage tech for good and think critically past the pitfalls. What Scilla put together for "The Creative Coping Toolkit" is a must-read for kids and families to help inform our behavior, decisions, and how we cope through these realities. More so, a guide of simple activities leading individuals through thinking and discussion routines that uncover the social and emotional complexities of living in an always-connected digital world. Encouraging authentic conversations and providing a space to reflect, is an essential practice for every home and everyone. Essentially, we need to disconnect in order to reconnect, and the CCT is a great guide in that practice."

**Merve Lapus**, Vice President & National Partnerships,
Common Sense Education

# TABLE OF CONTENTS

# FOREWORD

**Dr. Jerry Bubrick**
*Senior Psychologist, Child Mind Institute*

I WAS HONORED WHEN SCILLA ASKED ME TO WRITE THE foreword to this book. I mean, how sweet of her; with so many options, she chose me! Of course I was excited to do it for her.

I've written many professional articles, a book on anxiety, and even a comic book on obsessive compulsive disorder, but wait... I've never written a foreword before. How do you do it? What's the average word count? What should I talk about? What if I write something intended to be witty but someone takes offense to it? What if Scilla hates it and then resents me forever for ruining her book? What if, what if, what if...

So, naturally, I resorted to what any reasonable person would: how do I get out of it? Can I tell her I'm sick, or I broke my thumb in a freak psychologist accident? Then it occurred to me — read the table of contents and decide from there.

So I did. And wouldn't you know it, all the answers to my anxieties were right there. Activities like Comfort Words, Worry Jar, Doorway Affirmations, and 3 Breaths and 3 Wishes... I was instantly intrigued and, suddenly, much calmer. Reading the book and doing the exercises reminded me that I have the power to calm myself down and be in control when life seems chaotic.

**The Creative Coping Toolkit** is chock full of examples, strategies, inspirational quotes and games that people can play by themselves or with others, and is designed to inspire people to change the way they think, feel and do.

As a child psychologist specializing in anxiety disorders, I know this process very well (aside from my minor freak out mentioned earlier). The truth is anxiety disorders are real, common and treatable. Approximately 35% of children will have a diagnosable anxiety disorder by the age of 18, yet many of them will never receive treatment. This is a serious issue in the world and more needs to be done to raise awareness, decrease stigma, and make treatment more accessible. However, none of that is possible until we start the conversation. Scilla is doing just that. This book is an easy and fun way to start a conversation with a family member or a friend and inspire each other to think more rationally, change feelings and be happier.

Scilla really is an amazing person. She is a great friend, incredible filmmaker, awesome mom, daughter, sister and wife. She literally makes friends with everyone she meets, and now we can add to her list of accomplishments, a marvelous author.

---

### *About Dr. Jerry Bubrick*

*Jerry Bubrick, PhD, is a widely recognized cognitive and behavioral psychologist who specializes in the treatment of obsessive-compulsive disorder (OCD). He currently serves as Director of the Obsessive-Compulsive Disorder Service at the Child Mind Institute and is a frequent speaker at primary and secondary schools, academic medical centers, community health organizations and professional conferences. A dedicated advocate for children and their families, Dr. Bubrick is a significant public voice educating parents and teachers about the fear at the roots of anxiety — and how it's effectively treated.*

# INTRODUCING:
## *The Creative Coping Toolkit*

I NEVER DREAMED I WOULD CREATE A BOOK, BUT HERE IT IS.

It's been an extremely organic process. This book was written for the people I've met over the past 10 years who said they wished they had a guide or list of ways to better communicate, connect and talk about their feelings. I am not an expert nor a licensed professional in the world of mental health. I'm a mother, wife, daughter, sister, director, producer, CEO and friend whose mission in life is to help others feel like they matter, they belong, and they are enough just as they are.

I spent my early years feeling like I wasn't heard and I did not belong. I was silent. I didn't speak. My dad always said, "children should be seen and not heard." Don't get me wrong he was a good dad and very kind, it was just the times. I was never encouraged to use my voice. I was verbally, emotionally and physically bullied at school because I looked different. Being Chinese and Swedish in an all-white community in Breckenridge, Colorado I was literally the only kid of color in the whole county. So, I spent the first 12 years of my life trying to be invisible. I spent a lot of time observing everybody including myself. In my early twenties, I started to find my voice and while I struggled with debilitating feelings of anxiety and being overwhelmed; I taught myself to push through them, I had to. It wasn't until recently, when I was producing Angst, I learned that I have social anxiety. Fortunately, I also discovered that as a kid I'd developed some wonderful hacks for myself to navigate life with anxiety. I'm sharing some of them in this book.

I was inspired to write The Creative Coping Toolkit (CCT) after years of listening to the audience response to some of the films I produced and IndieFlix distributed like *Finding Kind, The Empowerment Project, Screenagers, Angst,* and *LIKE.* People would come up to me after screenings and tell me that they wanted a way to keep the conversation going at home. This consistent feedback of craving connection, coupled with my desire to share fun ways to find solutions and hone coping and communication skills, is the foundation of what has become The Creative Coping Toolkit (CCT).

Here with the help of Cole Weinstein and Natalie Andreen, who provided editorial support, and Jerrin Padre, an impressive young talent who is the author of *Bo & Whimsy* (a children's book on finding creative alternatives to screen time), a burgeoning filmmaker, brilliant thinker and this book's illustrator; we bring you, The Creative Coping Toolkit.

For those of you who know me, I love games and like to have fun with whatever I do. Talking about our feelings can sometimes be tough, so this book includes 10 simple activities that gamify talking about our emotions. You can do one or all of them anywhere — by yourself OR with a group (family, friends, classmates, band mates, book club, colleagues, tennis team, mahjong group etc.) Each exercise is easy to implement, peer-led, and appropriate for all ages. Have fun with it. Change it up. Customize it for you and your group. We hope you enjoy! It was written for you.

With love and gratitude,

Scilla xxoo

*25% of profits will be donated and shared with IndieFlix Foundation, Child Mind Institute, Seattle Children's Hospital and Z-Cares Foundation.*

# MOOD METER

My moods come and go
Just as the tides ebb and flow,
Yet I remain, still.


Jerrin Padre, *A Mood*

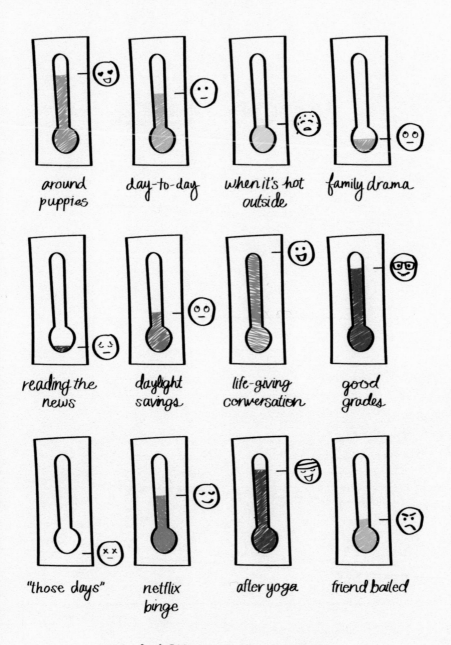

AN ANTHOLOGY OF MOODS

# MOOD METER

Sometimes it's easier to share how we're feeling by expressing it with a number. Choose a number between 1-10, 10 being great, and 1 being not good at all.

## *Rank your mood:*

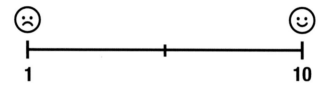

**THE GOAL:** *The goals of this exercise are to: 1) give everyone in the family a system for expressing their feelings, 2) understand the ways each family member prefers to be celebrated or comforted, and 3) normalize the conversation in a safe space. This can be done at breakfast, in the car, at dinner, or before bed!*

## MATERIALS:

- Something to write with
- Something to write on

# PART 1: GROUP ACTIVITY

**ASK**

Ask each member of the family to rank how they feel on a scale of 1-10 (10 being amazing, 1 being awful). Feel free to think of it on the spot or write it down.

**SHARE**

Once everybody's had the chance to rank their mood, go around the room and have each member of the family share their number.

**DISCUSS**

Have a group discussion! Go through each of the talking points below.

---

## TALKING POINTS

What events, thoughts, and people contribute to the way you are feeling right now?

What would you want someone to say or do if you felt like a 1 or 2? What about a 9 or 10?

How do you feel most comforted?

How do you like to celebrate?

How can we best help each other?

How can we better encourage each other?

Why do you think it's so hard to talk about how we are really feeling?

---

# PART 2: Individual Maintenance

 ## CHECK IN

Use the mood meter to assess how you're feeling on a regular basis, especially during times of stress or joy.

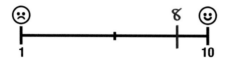

 ## DATE IT

Date each mood you record and add a brief description of what happened.

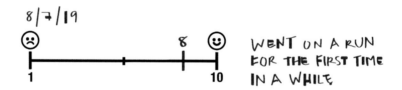

 ## REFLECT

Each month reflect on your recorded moods. Do you see any trends? Was it a really great month or a really stressful one? Taking time to reflect helps you see the bigger picture as you go through each season of life.

*Tip:* *If you notice you're feeling 0-5, reflect back on the days you were feeling 6-10 and take some tips for yourself.*

# TIPS FOR PARENTS

**Be vulnerable.** As parents, it's important to express your vulnerability. Don't be afraid to say you had a bad day at work.

**Wait to respond.** Though it may be tempting, refrain from responding, advising, or providing feedback to your kids *until they ask you for advice.* While you may think you're helping them solve the problem, unsolicited advice may exacerbate the issue as it doesn't give them the opportunity to properly process their emotions.

**Accept them as they are.** By not responding right away, you are showing your kid(s) that you accept them as they are. This is integral in getting them to a place where they feel ready to solve the problem.

**Sit with them.** While you're fighting the urge to respond, rescue, or fix, focus on sitting with your kiddo(s). It may be difficult, but simply sitting with someone in their sadness, anxiousness, anger, or any other negative emotion demonstrates that you are there for them (which is often what people need the most).

# 3 BREATHS & 3 WISHES

"I learned a long time ago that a person can stand just about anything for <u>10 seconds.</u>

Then you just start a <u>new</u> 10 seconds!

All you gotta' do is take it 10 seconds at a time."

**THE UNBREAKABLE**

*Kimmy Schmidt*

start

+10
sec

+10
sec

+10
sec

+10
sec

carry on

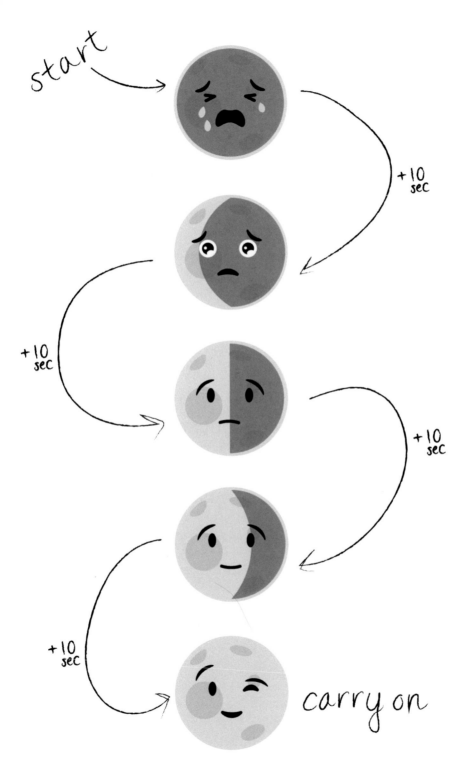

# DID YOU KNOW?

—

*How Breathing Hacks the Brain*

Researchers have found that breathing rhythms have a direct effect on brain activity[1]: the faster we breathe, the faster the activity in our brains. This increased activity is then able to influence our emotional states, which explains why people who are scared or stressed tend to hyperventilate (breathe at a fast pace), and why we're often told to take a deep breath when we need to calm down. Breathing changes the brain! So, the next time you feel frightened or worried, use the rhythm of your breath to hack your brain into following suit.

[1] *GoStrengths!*

# 3 BREATHS & 3 WISHES

We can all use a breather throughout the day — a way to ground and reconnect with ourselves and the people and places around us. Doing so doesn't always have to be an hour-long yoga class or 20-minute meditation. Sometimes all it takes is 30 seconds! Use this quick pick-me-up throughout the day to ground, reconnect, refocus, and remind yourself what matters.

**THE GOAL:** *To break the emotional circuit (when experiencing negative emotions) and find a sense of calm.*

## MATERIALS:

- Your lungs (and hopefully some clean air!)

# INSTRUCTIONS

## TAKE A STEP BACK

If you catch yourself feeling overwhelmed, in your head, or funky, stop what you're doing and take a step back. Then do the 3 Breaths & 3 Wishes. It only takes half a minute to find some calm.

### BREATH 1 IS FOR YOU

Count to 4 as you inhale, filling your lungs and diaphragm with as much air as you can. As you exhale, make a wish for yourself.

### BREATH 2 IS FOR ANOTHER PERSON

Count to 4 as you inhale, filling your lungs and diaphragm with as much air as you can. As you exhale, make a wish for that person.

### BREATH 3 IS FOR A COLLECTIVE

Count to 4 as you inhale, filling your lungs and diaphragm with as much air as you can. As you exhale, make a wish for the collective (family, classroom, country, etc).

## YOU'RE ALL DONE – CARRY ON!

3 breaths later and you're on your way! You've changed your brain. Feel free to repeat at any point in the day when you need to reground.

# COMFORT WORDS

When I need a hug,
And nobody's around,
I reach for my comfort words
To reboot and reground.


Jerrin Padre, *Comfort Words*

# DID YOU KNOW?

---

*Fight-or-flight Reactions*

Since the dawn of time, our brains have been hardwired to keep us safe.[2] At the first sign of danger, our nervous system sends our bodies into hyperdrive, preparing us to either fight off the threat (fight) or run away (flight). In life or death situations, this instinct can keep us alive, but what happens when our fight-or-flight response is triggered by everyday stressors?

See if you can recognize some of these fight-or-flight behaviors:

- Defensiveness or combativeness
- Avoidance
- Anxiousness
- Unhealthy distractions
- Placing blame
- Panic attacks

---

**Discussion Question:**
*When was the last time you felt/experienced one of the bullet points above? What caused you to feel that way?*

---

In order to manage fight-or-flight response, we need to train our brains to distinguish between real emergencies and everyday stressors. One way of doing so is to redirect your thinking. This is where Comfort Words come in!

[2] *Seattle Children's Hospital*

# COMFORT WORDS

Comfort Words are words to use when you feel stressed or bothered by something. They neutralize Fight-or-Flight words & feelings, which make your body think it's in a real emergency. Try to catch yourself before this happens by reaching for your Comfort Words to ground yourself.

**THE GOAL:** *The goal of this exercise is to equip you with a way to redirect your thinking before it gets out of hand.*

## MATERIALS:

- Comfort Words Chart (next page)
- Something to write with

# INSTRUCTIONS

### REVIEW

View the **_Comfort Words Chart_** on the next page (or print it out from the CCT Resource Page).

### BRAINSTORM

Using the prompts on the chart, have everyone brainstorm one word for each of the categories: Happy Place, Comfort Food, and a Person or Pet.

### WRITE IT DOWN

Fill out the Comfort Words Chart with everyone's Comfort Words. Then hang it on your fridge or some place where everyone can reference it!

### PRACTICE

Next time you feel your fight-or-flight response kicking in (without due cause), redirect your thinking by using one or all of your Comfort Words. Once you get into the habit of doing so, try helping others! If one of your family members needs redirecting, gently remind them of their Comfort Words. Talk about why they love that person/place/food. Ask them about other things that bring them joy!

# OUR COMFORT WORDS

Start by brainstorming a few comfort words for each category below.

| HAPPY PLACE |
| --- |
| A place that brings you joy! |

| FAVORITE FOOD |
| --- |
| Something you love to eat! |

| A SPECIAL PERSON, PET, OR OBJECT |
| --- |
| The name of a person, pet, or object that makes you smile! |

# FAMILY CHART

| NAME | COMFORT WORDS |
|------|---------------|
|      |               |
|      |               |
|      |               |
|      |               |
|      |               |
|      |               |
|      |               |
|      |               |

# 60 SECONDS OF THANKS

This is a wonderful day.
I've never seen this one before.

Maya Angelou

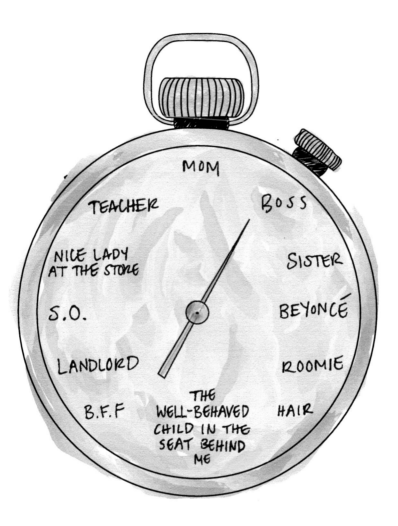

60 SECONDS OF THANKS

# DID YOU KNOW?

———

*The Power of Gratitude*

A simple and brief positive thought or emotion can change the brain and stretch the imagination. When we do something we enjoy or find interesting, we are more likely to persevere in the face of challenges and find more creative solutions and opportunities. Positive emotions can also help undo negative ones. Reminding ourselves about the good things in our life, no matter how big or small, offsets stress from a challenging day at school or work. A moment of gratitude, prayer or mindfulness are a few ways we can focus on positivity.[1]

[1]*GoStrengths!*

# 60 SECONDS OF THANKS

Sometimes taking a minute to reflect on the faces, places, and routines we tend to take for granted can make all the difference in changing our brains.

**THE GOAL:** *To get in the habit of making gratitude part of your day-to-day.*

## MATERIALS:

- Something to write with
- Something to write on

# INSTRUCTIONS

## REFLECT

For one minute, think of someone who has shown you a kindness or lent a helping hand.

## SAY THANK YOU

Thank that person! Write it down and share it with them. Or better yet —say it out loud! This practice changes your brain and promotes gratitude. It only takes half a minute to find some calm.

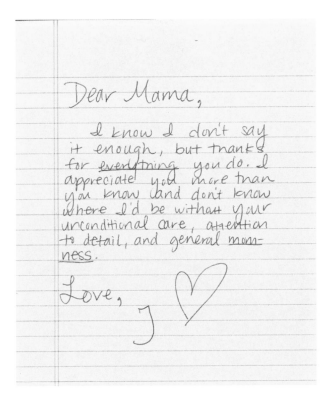

*The more gratitude we share, the more we have to be grateful for!*

# WORRY JAR

When we smile our organs relax.
When we laugh our soul breathes.


Scilla Andreen

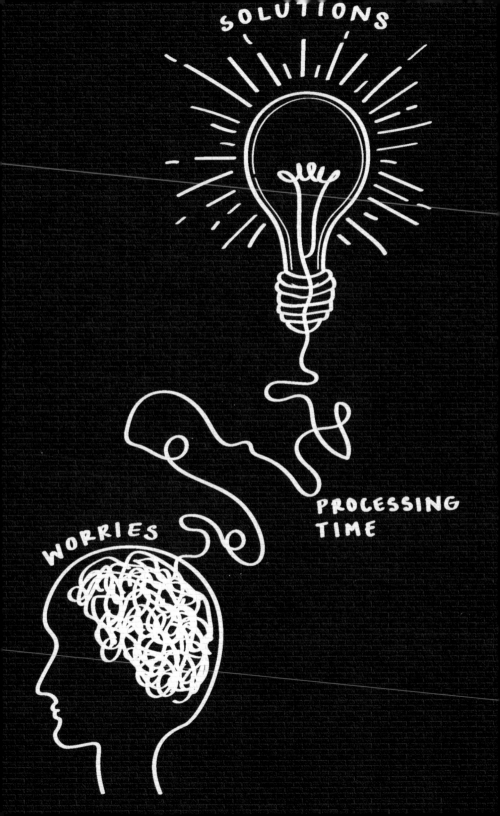

# DID YOU KNOW?

———

*Leading By Example*

According to experts, modeling the behavior we want from our kids, parents, co-workers and friends is much more effective than complaining or talking about it.[3] Therefore, when kids see their parents, grandparents and friends **talk about things they're going through** and **engage in enjoyable, yet challenging, activities to find creative solutions**, they see the contentment it brings and are more likely to model the same behavior (be it in sports, academics, music or social settings).

[3]*Positive Psychology Center, University of Pennsylvania*

# WORRY JAR

Sometimes writing down our worries can make all the difference. By acknowledging the things that make us anxious, we're one step closer to finding a solution. Use this exercise to manage your worries and watch them turn into solutions.

**THE GOAL:** *To develop a productive way of managing worries and anxious feelings.*

## MATERIALS:

- 2 mason jars or any other jar (old pasta jars work wonders!)
- notecards/scrap paper
- writing utensil
- tape

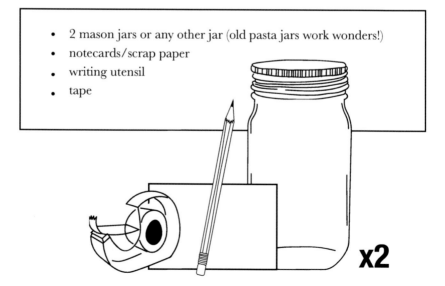

**x2**

# INSTRUCTIONS

## PREP

Once you've gathered the materials, make a group Worry Jar and group Solution Jar. Take 2 notecards or pieces of scrap paper and write "worry jar" and "solution jar" on each. Tape these labels onto the two jars.

## WRITE

Pass out notecards, sticky notes, or pieces of scrap paper to the group. Ask everyone to write down things that stress them out, worry them, or make them anxious (one worry per card). Then have them fold up their worries and drop them in the "worry jar."

## TAKE SOME TIME

Feel free to dive right in (see "REVISIT & BRAINSTORM" on next page) OR take some time. It could be a day, a week, a month — whatever's most comfortable for you. Taking time forces everyone to take the crucial step of feeling their feelings.

# Instructions (cont.)

### REVISIT & BRAINSTORM

Revisit the worries with everyone or with one other person (again, whatever makes you feel most comfortable). Have a volunteer pick a worry out of the jar and read it aloud. Then have everyone brainstorm creative ways to manage or move past that particular worry! Write them down on the back of the original worry card. Repeat this a few times!

Worry:
Geometry test on
Monday

Solution:
Study group on
Sunday w/ friends

### GROW THE SOLUTION JAR

Keep the "solution jar" right next to the "worry jar." After brainstorming ways to push through or manage a worry, add them to the "solution jar." Watch as the solutions build and the worries, hopefully, go down.

## TIPS:

- *Make sure to space out your brainstorming session — do a couple worry/solutions at a time!*
- *If the group gets stumped on a worry, give it some more time! You can always come back to it later.*
- *Save the solutions that you can use in the future!*

# DOORWAY
# AFFIRMATIONS

A friend once told me, "Everytime
you walk through a door,
say something positive
about your life."


Michael Phelps

# DOORWAY AFFIRMATIONS

Doors symbolize new beginnings; out with the old, in with the new! Let doorways serve as opportunities for mini-beginnings and moments of positivity throughout your day.

**THE GOAL:** *To give you a little dose of mindfulness and a dash of positive affirmation in your day-to-day routine.*

## MATERIALS:

- A doorway

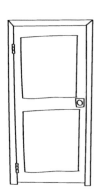

# INSTRUCTIONS

## FORM A HABIT

Every time you go through a doorway, say one of the following:

**something nice about yourself**

**something nice about your day**

**something nice about someone in your life**

*If you can't think of something positive on the spot, just say the words "gratitude," "joy," "happiness," or even, "I'm OK."*

# KNOW YOUR SELF(IE)

One thing I see is people are actually starting to show more of themselves online. And I think that's a great thing. Sometimes they're showing the great moments, but then sometimes they're also showing their struggles. And if we see someone that sounds like they're struggling, I think it's important to really pay attention to that. To hear them. And if you think it's necessary... Feel free to tell someone. Or ask them about it, or engage with them. Because usually those are cries for help. And it's our job, as people who see it, to answer those cries.

Leah Pearlman,
Co-creator of Facebook "Like" Button/
Creator of Dharma Comics

# DID YOU KNOW?

---

*Building Community On and Offline Can
Spread Positive Emotions*

Humans are social beings. According to research, engaging with people in person and online can spread contagious emotions.[3] Happiness, laughter and a sense of community can all be passed along, but so can feelings of hurt and negativity. The kindness and respect we're taught to show others offline should be practiced online as well.

Additionally, children are 1 in 5 times more likely to share their feelings with peers and friends rather than adults.[4] As humans, we tend to measure our successes and general quality of life through points of comparison to others of a similar age. Therefore, adults must learn to respect the relationships fostered by their children, younger siblings, or students by giving them the space to share their feelings however and with whomever they choose, while also letting them know they are always there for them.

[3] *Positive Psychology Center, University of Pennsylvania*
[4] *Center for Healthy Minds, University of Wisconsin-Madison*

# KNOW YOUR SELF(IE)

It's easy to get lost in the noise of our never-ending social media feeds. Discover how to cultivate the best social media experience for you with this value-finder activity!

**THE GOAL:** *The goal of this exercise is to create a happier, healthier, and more purposeful social media experience for each individual by fostering the same quality of interactions and relationships online as offline— It's an exercise in self-compassion!*

## MATERIALS:

- List of questions (next page)
- Something to write with
- Something to write on

# INSTRUCTIONS

## ANSWER

Answer the prompts on the following page.

> Tip: Write your answers down in a place where you can refer back to them later, like a journal or planner!

## REFLECT

Ask yourself how each answer can inform how you use social media going forward. Are you posting to *give*? Or are you posting to *get*?

> **Tip:** If you're doing this activity as a family, go through each question and have everyone answer individually. Before moving onto the next question, have a group discussion about how everyone's answers inform how they could interact with social media going forward.
>
> ***For example:*** If someone were to answer Question 1 (see prompt on next page) with "Spreading Kindness," then perhaps they could try posting a photo of someone they admire with a caption about why they admire them. Or maybe they start to follow people and accounts that also spread kindness.

## INCORPORATE

Encourage everyone to keep their answers in mind whenever they go on social media.

# DISCUSSION PROMPTS

Feel free to jot down your ideas in the blue boxes!

**1. What's something you want to be known for?** *(Use this to inform what/how you will post on social media.)*

> **Examples:** giving the best hugs, making movies, beautiful drawings, making yummy food, being an upstander

**2. What's one positive thing you wish you could share with the world?** *(Use this to inform what/how you will post on social media.)*

> **Examples:** tips on how to have a productive conversation, expressions of kindness, music, healthy living, my bug collection

**3. List 3 things that make you happy.** *(Use this to inform what and who you interact with or follow on social media.)*

> **Examples:** french bulldogs, cat videos, watermelon, people playing with slime, the beach, memes

**4. List 3 things you want to learn more about.** *(Use this to inform what/how you will post on social media.)*

> **Examples:** how to keep the planet healthy, mindfulness, nature, parenting tips, fashion

**5. What are 3 things you could do to truly connect with someone over social media?** *(Use this to inform how you'll foster meaningful relationships over social media.)*

> **Examples:** DM (direct message) them a compliment or question on something they posted that you want to learn more about

# FRIENDLY PHRASES

What if I fall?
Oh, but my darling, what if you fly?


Erin Hanson,
Poet

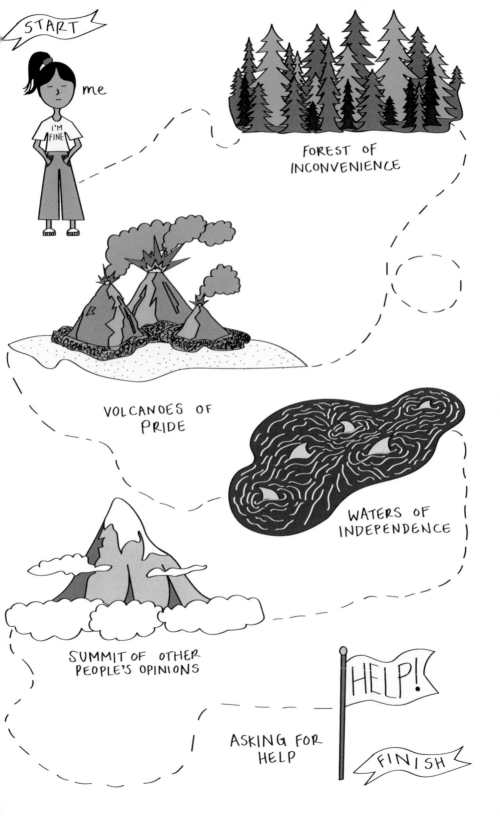

# FRIENDLY PHRASES

Sometimes speaking up is hard, especially in times of high stress, anxiety, grumpiness, etc. The same goes for responding to someone in a similar mental state. Friendly Phrases are conversation starters anyone can use to self-advocate or advocate for others when life is throwing lemons.

**THE GOAL:** *The goal of this exercise is to equip you with a way to redirect your thinking before it gets out of hand.*

## MATERIALS:

- Friendly Phrases Worksheet (next page)
- Something to write with (optional)
- Something to write on (optional)

# INSTRUCTIONS

## REVIEW

If you're going through this activity alone, review the **Friendly Phrases** (next page). If you're going through this activity as a family and would like to print out sheets for everyone:

> **1.** Visit the **CCT Resources Page** (link in the back of this book)
>
> **2.** Download the **Friendly Phrases Worksheet**
>
> **3.** Print it out and distribute to the group OR save some paper and display it on a laptop, monitor, or tv where everyone can read!

## BRAINSTORM

Once you have time to review, brainstorm some other phrases you could potentially say for each scenario. Write them down!

> **Tip:** If in a group or family setting, *have a conversation* about each of the three scenarios. What other responses could be appropriate for each?

## APPLY

Be on the lookout for scenarios your Friendly Phrases may come in handy. You may just make someone's day!

> **Tip:** Feel free to role play! The more you practice asking for help, the easier it will become.

# FRIENDLY PHRASES WORKSHEET

Explore a few scenarios where Friendly Phrases may come in handy. Then brainstorm some of your own in the area provided.

## *When You're Going Through a Hard Time and Want to Ask for Help*

*"Hey, do you have a second? Working through some stuff and need to vent."*

*"Hey, could I get your perspective on something?"*

*"I'm having a tough day, can I talk to you?"*

*"I could really use some friend time, do you have a minute?"*

**Your Ideas:**

## *When You See Someone Else Going Through a Hard Time*

*"Hey, _____, Here to lend an ear, if you need. No pressure though!"*

*"Can I sit with you?"*

*"Need anything?"*

**Your Ideas:**



## *When Someone Tells You What They're Going Through*

*"Gosh, I can't imagine."*

*"That sounds like a lot."*

*"That makes sense."*

*"Thanks for opening up to me!"*

**Your Ideas:**

# BEDTIME SEEDS

Water the flowers,
not the weeds.


Scilla Andreen

# DID YOU KNOW?

——

*The Benefits of Daily Reflection*

Neuroplasticity (i.e. the brain's ability to form and reorganize itself) is real. Any time we learn or experience something new, our brains generate new connections, produce new cells, as well as sculpt existing thinking patterns, all in the effort to help us be more efficient.[4]

We can shape our brains in beneficial ways by cultivating healthy mind habits such as **daily reflection**.[5] Taking some time at the end of each day to note the good that happens in our lives trains our brain to remember that, even on tough days, life *can* be sweet. Plus, making daily reflection a habit may also make for sweeter dreams!

[4] *Center for Healthy Minds, University of Wisconsin-Madison*
[5] *University of Pennsylvania and the John Templeton Foundation*

# BEDTIME SEEDS

Research has shown that some of the most successful people reflect on their day before they go to bed.[6] By taking time to acknowledge the day's positive events (no matter how mundane), we're reminded that life, in all it's zany ways, is working on our behalf. Use this bedtime ritual as a way to wind down and sow your own seeds of motivation.

**THE GOAL:** *To make sure the tiny nuggets of inspiration, joy, wisdom, and lessons learned don't go unaccounted for.*

## MATERIALS:

- Something to write with (we recommend a journal so you can look back at old seeds you've planted)
- Something to write on

[6] *Michael Kerr*

# INSTRUCTIONS

## WRITE & REFLECT

Before you go to bed, write down three things that went right today **and why.**
They can be anything from 3 things you appreciate to 3 things you learned.
Do this every night before bed.

> **NOTE:** Adding the "why" is especially important as it kicks your
> metacognition into gear. You won't tire of the exercise as quickly
> and will be far more likely to build similar conditions that enable
> thriving or strength-based situations in the future.

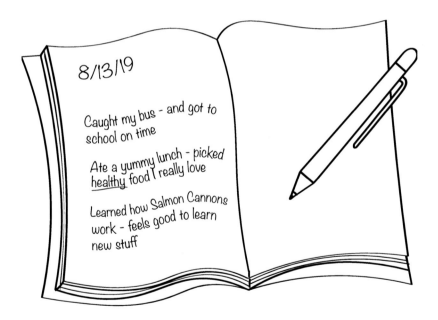

Every day, there are at least a few things that either went right or were learned.
Hindsight is 20/20, so, if you find yourself in the thick of it, put your focus on
the good stuff until it shines so bright the darkness begins to fade.

# FUN FACT

**"Your brain at positive is 31% more productive** than your brain at negative, neutral or stressed."

Shawn Achor

# GOOD HEARTED LIVING

I like living. I have sometimes been wildly, despairingly, acutely miserable, racked with sorrow; but through it all I still know, quite certainly, that just to be alive is a grand thing.

Agatha Christie

# DID YOU KNOW?

———

*The Science of Well-being*

The human brain is resilient. Throughout our life, the brain is constantly re-wiring, growing and adapting. Due to its quick ability to change in response to experience and training, research suggests that, in the same way we can learn an instrument, we can also learn *well-being*.[4]

According to Merriam-Webster, **well-being** is defined as "the state of being happy, healthy, or prosperous." It is associated with numerous health, job, family, and socioeconomic-related benefits such as a decreased risk of disease, illness, and injury; better immune system functioning; speedier recovery; and increased longevity.

[4] *Center for Healthy Minds, University of Wisconsin-Madison*

# GOOD HEARTED LIVING

(Special thanks to Dr. Cora Breuner and Seattle Children's Hospital)[7]

**Good Hearted Living** is the act of adding laughter and positivity into your life by minimizing attitudes and behaviors that promote stress:

- fear
- worry
- anger
- inflexibility
- perfectionism
- competitiveness
- holding grudges
- being judgmental
- etc.

Use this week-long challenge to help cultivate a sense of Good Hearted Living each day!

**THE GOAL:** *To help you and the family develop tactics that add more joy (and less stress) to your routines.*

## MATERIALS:

- A Week of Good Hearted Living poster (next page)
- Chocolate (optional)

# INSTRUCTIONS

## REVIEW

Review the **Good Hearted Living Poster** found on the next page or the CCT Resource Page (link in the back of the book).

> **Tip:** If you're feeling crafty, try re-drawing the poster on a larger poster board!

## LEAD THE TROOPS

Find some time at the beginning of each day to review that day's Good Hearted Living focus (Compliments, Flexibility, etc.). Then have a quick discussion about potential ways that focus could play out in day-to-day life!

## REFLECT

At the end of each day, gather as a group and reflect on everyone's experiences. Ask each other: What did you learn? What brought you the most joy? How were your stress levels?

This can be done at dinner or before bed!

# A WEEK OF GOOD HEARTED LIVING

**MON**

Compliments

Mondays are for compliments. Compliments are gifts (and they're free)! On Mondays, look for the good in yourself and other people and pay them a compliment whenever possible.

**Discussion:** Talk about the last compliment you received and the last compliment you gave.

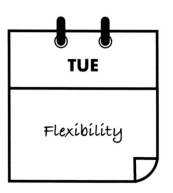

**TUE**

Flexibility

Tuesdays are for flexibility. Today, your challenge is to try something new. Be open! Eat something different, listen to a new song, try a new fitness class... Break out of the norm and be flexible! Doing so helps break patterns and allows you to discover new things about yourself.

**WED**

Gratitude

On Wednesdays, we wear gratitude! Be thankful for what you have today. Pay attention to both the wins (no matter how small) and the challenges. Then, before everyone goes to bed, get together as a family and share 3 things that went right today. Just as we learned in 60 Seconds of Thanks, consistently practicing gratitude gives us a new sense of grounding and perspective.

**THU**

*Kindness*

Whether it's holding a door, helping with the dishes, or just listening, sometimes doing the smallest thing for someone can make their day. Today, focus on doing small things that'll make someone's life easier (e.g. cook your family a meal, help someone carry their groceries, run an errand for someone, etc).

**FRI**

*Forgiveness*

Let go of old, unpleasant thoughts today. Be forgiving — to others and especially yourself. Let go of grudges, shame, guilt, and any other negative emotions or thoughts that put you in a funky headspace. Hopefully, it'll help you clear the way for more joy, wisdom, and laughter.

**SAT/SUN**

*Chocolate\**

\*Or anything else that makes life sweet for you! Weekends are for good, old-fashioned TLC, so kick back, relax, and do things you enjoy guilt-free (like eating chocolate). Be playful! Doodle, have a dance party, watch a movie, blow bubbles, or sing in the shower.

**Discussion:** Brainstorm some activities that you can do as a family over the weekend!

# RESOURCES

# RESOURCE LIST

Scan this QR code to visit the CCT Resource List!

SCAN ME

# REFERENCES

**1.** "What is PERMA?" *GoStrengths!* https://gostrengths.com/whatisperma/. Accessed October 2019.

**2.** "Neutral Words." *Seattle Children's: Patient and Family Education*, 2015, Seattle Children's Hospital.

**3.** "Positive Psychology Center." *University of Pennsylvania.* https://ppc.sas.upenn.edu/. Accessed October 2019.

**4.** "Learning Well-being." Center for Healthy Minds, *University of Wisconsin-Madison.* https://centerhealthyminds.org/science/studies/learning-well-being. Accessed October 2019.

**5.** "Positive Neuroscience." *University of Pennsylvania.* http://posneuroscience.org/. Accessed October 2019.

**6.** Kerr, Michael. *You Can't Be Serious! Putting Humor to Work.* Speaking of Ideas, June 2001.

**7.** "Good Hearted Living." *Seattle Children's: Patient and Family Education*, 2015, Seattle Children's Hospital.

# ABOUT
# THE AUTHOR

# Scilla Andreen
*Author*

*Photo by Coco Knudson*

Scilla, (Pronounced Sheila) is an Emmy nominated award-winning TV and film industry veteran with 25+ years of experience working at several major film studios including Sony and Warner Bros before co-founding IndieFlix, a global, streaming and screening distribution service that focuses on content for a purpose. She's Included in Screening International's Women To Watch, Variety's Women's Impact Report, PSBJ Women of Influence and is a popular speaker at Sundance, Cannes, CES, SIC, SXSW, Women in Film, Hong Kong Mental Health Summits and other major industry events. She most recently directed The Upstanders and LIKE and is an Executive Producer of social impact films such as, Nevertheless, Angst and Screenagers. Her movies screen in thousands of schools, corporations and organizations throughout the world. She resides with her blended family of 6 kids and 2 dogs in Seattle, WA.

Scilla is on a mission to change the world with film. To learn more about her work, visit: indieflix.com

# ABOUT THE ILLUSTRATOR

## *Jerrin Padre*
*Designer/Illustrator*

*Photo by Stuart Danford*

Jerrin Padre is a consultant, writer, actor, and artist based out of Los Angeles, CA. Born and raised in sunny San Diego, Jerrin found an early love for storytelling through her involvement in performing arts. Upon entering college at the University of Washington, Jerrin intentionally shifted trajectories and graduated with a Bachelor's of Science in Speech and Hearing Sciences and a minor in Entrepreneurship. While her background and experience span a broad range of skills and industries, much of Jerrin's work centers around a deep love of storytelling. She often refers to her work saying, "There's this confusing, yet thrilling, intersection where art meets business, strategy meets creativity, visual design meets communication, and storytelling finds a purpose. That's where I like to be!" In addition to the CCT, Jerrin published <u>Bo & Whimsy</u>, a children's book geared toward helping parents and kids find creative alternatives to screen time. To learn more about Jerrin's work visit: <u>jerrinpadre.com</u> or <u>boandwhimsy.com</u>

# ABOUT INDIEFLIX

## IndieFlix Group, Inc.
*Seattle, WA*

IndieFlix Group, Inc. is an American entertainment company offering global screening and streaming distribution services that promote and support social impact films to create positive change in the world. Through their screening services, IndieFlix organizes offline community screenings in schools, corporations and communities around the world. Additionally, their streaming service offers a monthly subscription to access thousands of high-quality shorts, features, documentaries, and series from 85 countries, hundreds of film festivals and the top film schools. To learn more visit: www.indieflix.com


## IndieFlix Foundation
*Seattle, WA*

IndieFlix Foundation is a 501(c)(3) that promotes and supports social impact films and curriculum to create positive change in the world. These programs screen directly in schools and communities to foster conversation at the family level and nurture a more social, emotional, empathetic culture. To learn more visit: indieflixfoundation.org

# ACKNOWLEDGEMENTS

This book is inspired and made possible because of the unwavering support, encouragement, honesty and love of dear friends, family and colleagues who have always stood by me even when the rest of the world thought I was crazy.

Thank you to my partner in life, Eric Winn; our children Ian Andreen, Natalie Andreen, Ally Winn, Arin Winn, Jesse Winn, and Rashel Winn; my mom Mei-Ling Andreen; my family Maili, Ken, Jack, Stella and Lily Lafayette, Ann Wong, Lee Andreen, Pat Sheldon, Belinda Brackenridge, and JC Rudolph; my friends and colleagues Karin Gornick, Jolene McCaw, Aurelie McKinstry, Craig Stewart, Dr. Cora Breuner, Dr. Jerry Bubrick, Dr. Emily Wong, Dr. Laura Kastner, Dr. Martin Seligman, Rose Kauper, Dr. Bernd Friedlander, Karyn and Joe Barer, Spafford Robbins, Bart Hutchinson, Sarah Moga Alemany, Greg Moga, Cole Weinstein, Liberty Tanghal, Ann Skrobut, Zak Groner, Lisa Anderson, Andrea Downie, Elizabeth, Bill, and Harry Kahane, Coco Knudson, Pamela Otto, Andrea Lieberman, Shelley Callaghan, Jules Frazier, Leslie Chihuly, Maria and Kevin Cahoon, Ruth True, Julie Johnston, Jim Pruitt, Barbara Malone, Judy Bingham, Eliza Shelden, Rob and Robin McKenzie, Andrew McKenzie, Tom Meadowcroft, Sheila Fitzgerald, Jimmy Eland, Chris and Mary Karges, Mark and Erin Callaghan, Tommy Marquez, Cindy and Brent Bostwick, Abra and Timm Miller, Julienne Kuttel, Susanne Pruitt, Jens Molbak, Tucker Tooley, Patti Payne, Linda Wyman, Ali Mohsenian, Caron Carlyon, Kathleen Caldwell, Martha Moseley, Patti Brooke, Betty Tong, Lauren Selig, Robin Gainey, Denise Muyco, Jennifer Reibman, Tom and Julie Skerritt, Leah Pearlman, Max Stossel, Blair and John Borthwick, T Clark, Nicole Jon Sievers, Lauren and Aaron Paul, Molly Thompson, Sarah Moshman, Dana Michelle Cook, Dana and Nelson McCormick, Dan Gieschen, Paul and Dina Pigott, Carlo and Eulalie Scandiuzzi, Steven and Linda Levine; and last but not least, Tina Helsell who launched me on this journey of delving deep into mental and physical wellness and sharing it with the world. Thank you. Together we can do anything!

# YOU ARE HERE.

# YOU GOT THIS!
## :)

Made in the USA
Monee, IL
11 December 2019